better together*

*This book is best read together, grownup and kid.

 akidsco.com

a
kids
book
about

a kids book about

JOY

by Shivantika Jain Kothari

a
kids
book
about

Printed in the United States of America.

A Kids Book About books are available online: *akidsco.com*

To share your stories, ask questions, or inquire about bulk
purchases (schools, libraries, and nonprofits), please use
the following email address: *hello@akidsco.com*

Print ISBN: 978-1-958825-97-6
Ebook ISBN: 978-1-958825-98-3

Designed and illustrated by Shivantika Jain Kothari
Edited by Jennifer Goldstein and Emma Wolf

To the child who lives within us, long after we are all grown up. And to my parents, for giving me a childhood filled with love, safety, and joy.

Intro

You might be wondering why joy is important enough to write a book about. Well, joy is serious business.

Joy is about more than just being happy for a fleeting moment. It's a reminder that there is hope in the world, even in the hardest of times. Joy can be found while overcoming challenges, learning from mistakes, and helping people.

Joy is about connecting with people. Regardless of our ethnicity, age, or gender, we feel joy in the same, simple ways, and a smile is the same in every language. To feel joy is to be human.

As a result, joy helps us improve relationships, increase confidence, reduce stress, and fight depression. It helps us live longer and be our best selves.

As kids, we feel unapologetic, uninhibited joy. As we grow up, joy can often be trivialized, deprioritized or even forgotten. So grownups, as you read this book with the kid in your life, remember that this is an invitation for you, too—to find joy, hold onto it, and never let it go.

Hello!

I have a secret to share with you.

There's something you're *really* good at, and you probably don't even know it.

You might even be better at it than most of the grownups around you.

Some might say...
it's your
SUPERPOWER.

Do you want to
know what it is?

It's a little
something
called...

JOY.*

*Except it's not always so little. You'll see.

When you are a kid,
it's easier to feel excited
or happy about things,
without even realizing it.

Like when you play your favorite game or eat something you LOVE.

Do you know the happy feeling
I'm talking about?

That's...

Hi! I'm JOY. I'm everywhere, if you really look. See if you can spot me on every page!

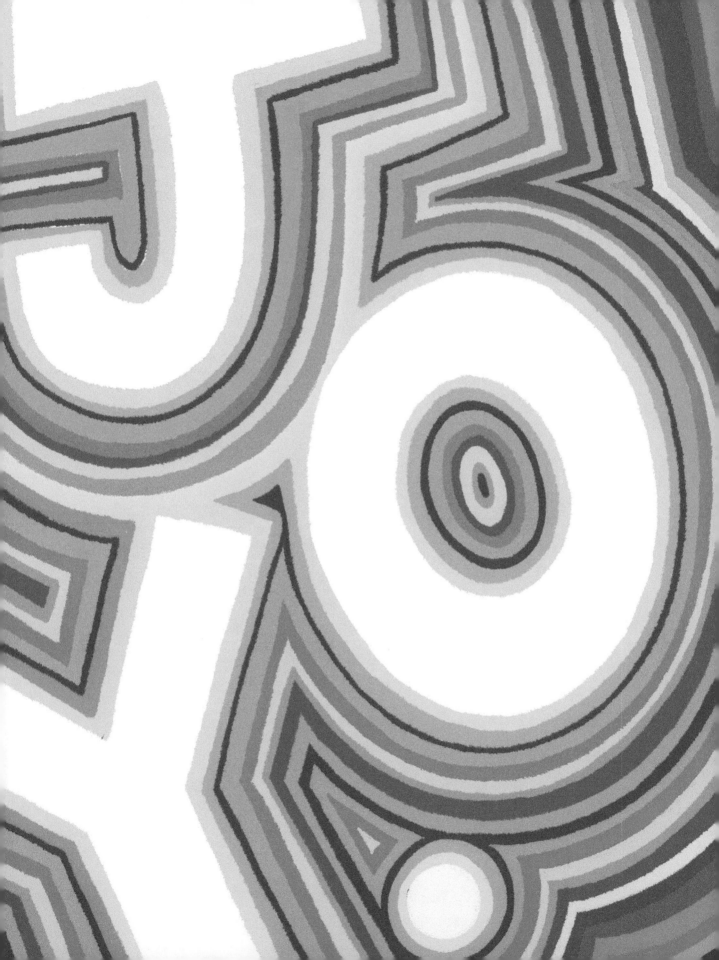

But here's the interesting part:

To Do LIST
• Laundry

• Thin
excuses
the gym

Sometimes as we grow up, joy might feel harder to find.

It may seem like there are so many, more important things in life to focus on, that we forget about joy.

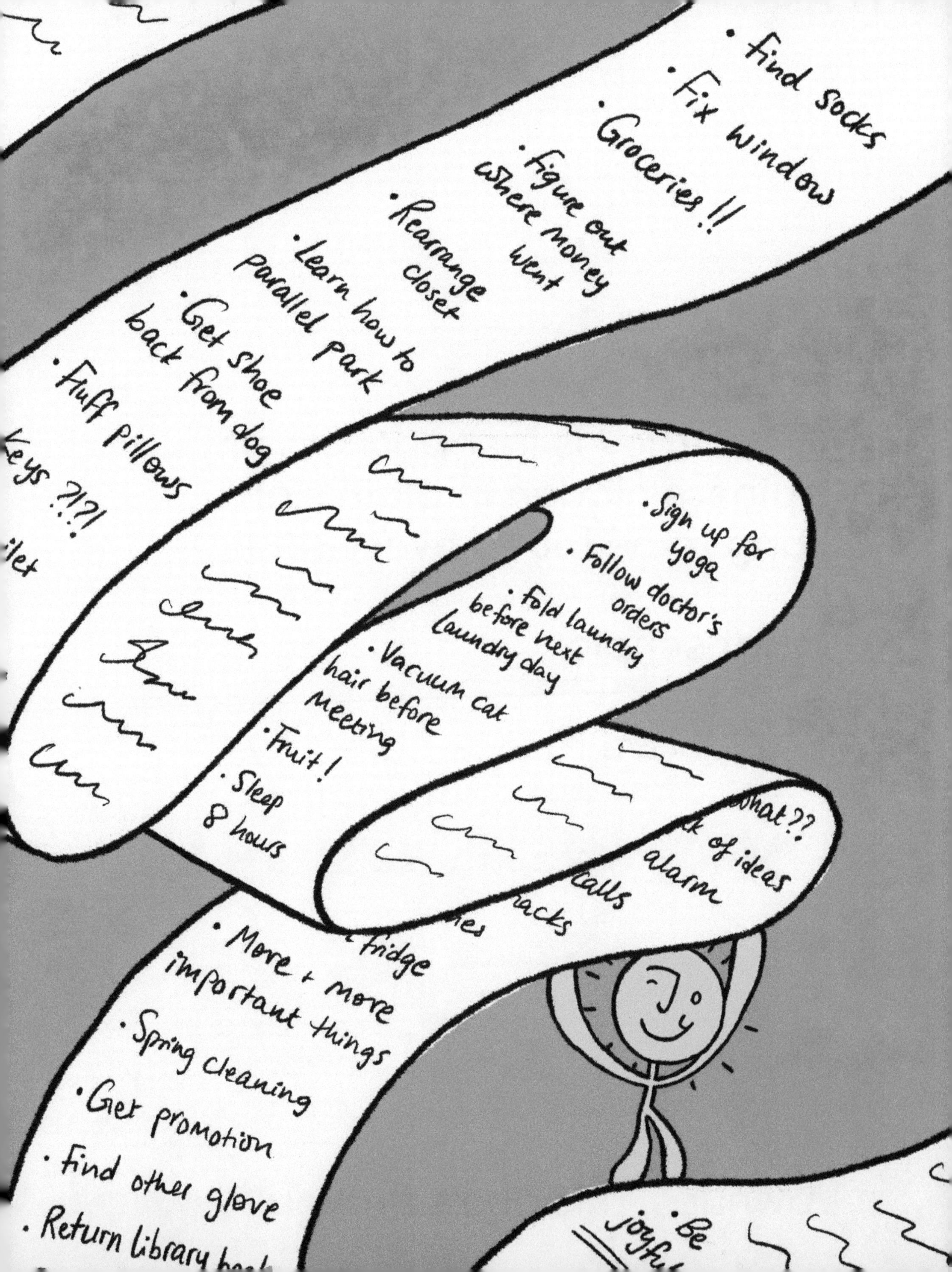

• find socks
• Fix window
• Groceries !!
• figure out where money went
• Rearrange closet
• Learn how to parallel park
• Get shoe back from dog
• Fluff pillows
Keys ?!?!
• Sign up for yoga
• Follow doctor's orders
• fold laundry before next laundry day
• Vacuum cat hair before meeting
• Fruit!
• Sleep 8 hours
alarm
calls
fridge
• More + more important things
• Spring cleaning
• Get promotion
• find other glove
• Return library
• Be joyful

But really, joy is just pockets of happiness hidden in plain sight, waiting to be found every day!

It's that simple.

You just have to look carefully.*

*Grownups, this one's for you!

Joy can be

or

It can be hiding where you least expect it.

EVERYONE CAN FEEL JOY

It's a big part of what makes us human, and what connects us.

Have you ever noticed that when you see someone smiling, you smile?

Or when you hear someone laughing, you feel like laughing too?

HA
ha
ha
ha
ha
ha
HAHAHA
HAHA
HA
HA
HA
HOHOHAHAH
HAHEHEHEHAH
HAHAHAHA
ha
HAHA
HAHA
HOHAHAHA
HAHAHA

It doesn't matter if that person is a kid, or a very very old person, or someone who speaks a different language...

it still works!

Want to know why?

Because it's contagious!
(But not in an icky way.)

c c c

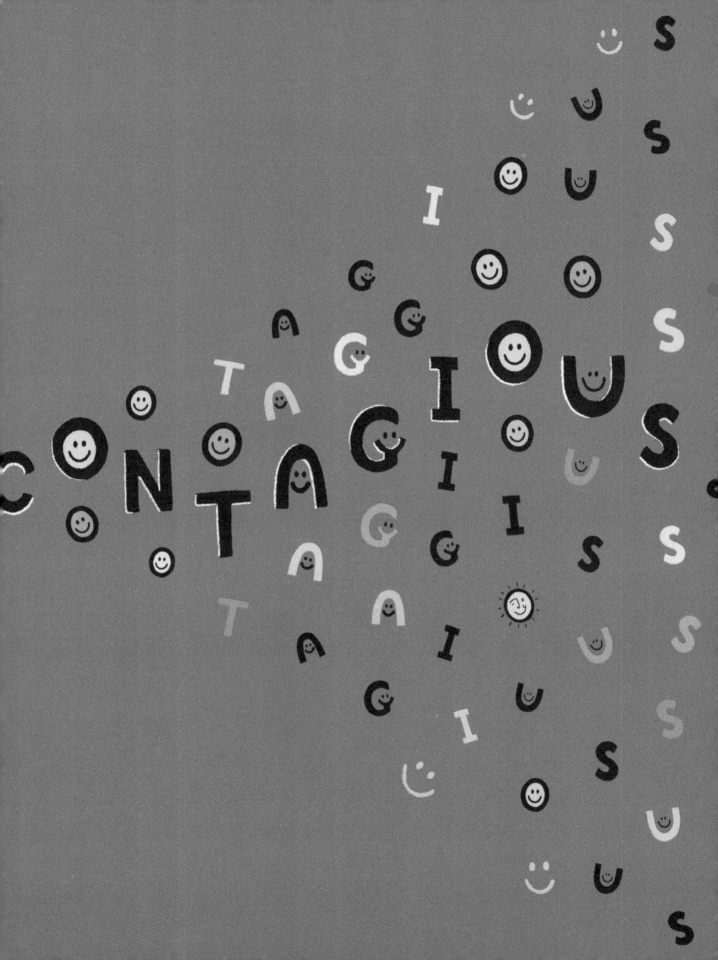

Joy is easy to share, and we can feel joy when we are kind and helpful to others.

Joy is something that doesn't become smaller when it's shared.

It's not like a pizza!
(Although for me, they're pretty much the same thing.)

But here's a funny thing:

EVEN THOUGH WE CAN ALL FEEL JOY, it CAN mean something DIFFERENT TO EACH of US.

For some people,
joy looks like this:

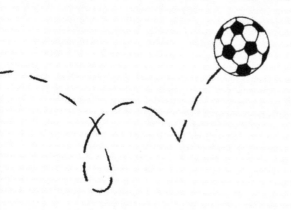

For others,
joy looks like this:

FOR ME, JOY LOOKS
LIKE THIS:

WHAT DOES JOY
LOOK LIKE FOR YOU?

If you're not sure, try thinking about some things that:

give you a warm, fuzzy feeling in your tummy,

or make you smile from ear to ear,

or make you want to laugh...
or make funny noises...
or shout at the top of your lungs (in a happy way!).

OK. Now that you know what joy can be and just how BIG it is, I have something very important to tell you.

BEING JOYFUL

BEING HAPPY

DOES NOT MEAN

ALL THE TIME

It also does not mean that you won't ever feel sad, or angry, or frustrated, or scared.

You are human, and that's what humans do.

We feel all kinds of things, and we can't always help it.

WHAT WE DO

WITH THAT FEELING

IS OUR CHOICE.

The real magic happens when we choose to find joy even when we're feeling crummy (...especially when we're feeling crummy!).

Because even though we can't always make the yucky stuff go away, we can **ALWAYS** choose to find j😊y in the smallest of ways, if we set our mind to it.

When you
are stressed,
you can still
find joy.

When you are
angry or frustrated
or sick or tired, you
can still find joy.

When you are sad, you can still find joy.

LET ME TELL YOU HOW:

NOTICE JOY.

As you go about your day, start to notice what activities, things, or people make you feel that happy feeling inside.

Every time you think of one, write it down and put it in a jar. Collect as many as you can!

Step 2:

CHOOSE JOY.

The next time you're feeling down, pull an idea out of your Joy Jar. And then, go do that thing!

Better yet, why wait for when you're down? You can do this every day!

Doing activities that bring joy also helps you reduce stress and feel confident.*

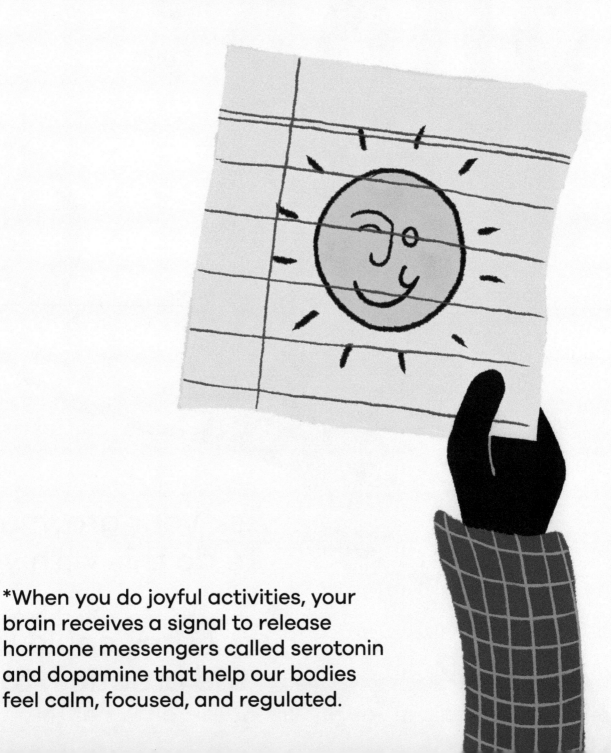

*When you do joyful activities, your brain receives a signal to release hormone messengers called serotonin and dopamine that help our bodies feel calm, focused, and regulated.

Step 3:

SHARE JOY.

Ask your grownups
to do this with you.

(They could use
the practice, too!)

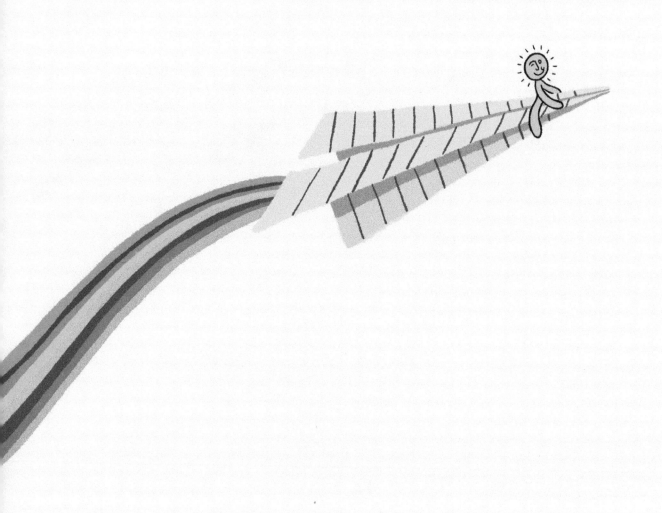

They can make their own
Joy Jar, or pick from
yours. You can help them
remember how important
joy is, and how easily they
can choose to have it in
their lives.

When people feel good and happy inside, it helps them feel kindness toward themselves and others. They then help spread it around and before you know it, the world is a more joyful place!

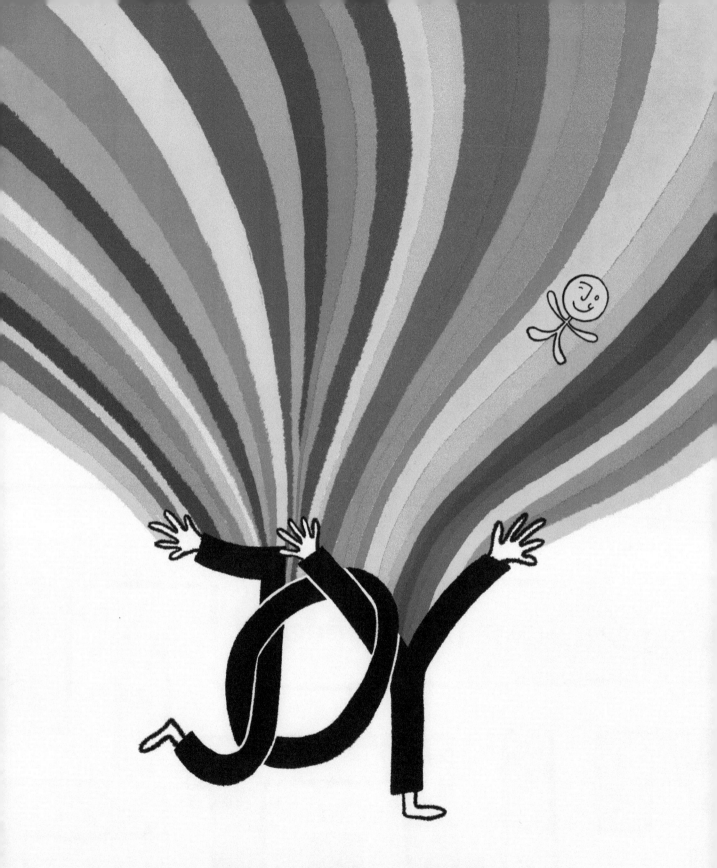

How great is that?

So, it's settled.
Joy is serious
business.

can be felt by anyone

It

It is simple to find.

yet can

be different for everyone. We can choose (and spread) it every day.

Go on, now—what are you waiting for?!

Joy is your superpower!

Outro

I hope this book has brought you some moments of joy, and above all, I hope it encourages you to make more room for joy every day.

Now that you know that there are about a zillion ways to find joy (even in the hard times!), it is important to remember these 3 points:

1. Joy is everywhere, and can be found even when you least expect it.

2. Being joyful does not mean being falsely happy all the time. Joy can exist along with all kinds of crummy feelings.

3. Joy is a choice. We can't always change the things happening around us, but we can choose to find joy in spite of them.

Here's wishing you a Joy Jar that overflows for the years to come. And if you haven't started yours yet...what are you waiting for?!

About The Author

When Shivantika (she/her) was little, she and her best friend wanted to start a Happiness Factory. The machines in the factory would produce little bottles of happiness, which people could take home and use to solve whatever problems they had. It was going to be amazing.

What they soon learned was that happiness didn't have to be manufactured. It was already available in abundance, hidden all over the world, and could be found in the simplest ways. These little moments of happiness are called joy, and they're surprisingly easy to find!

Shivantika wrote this book to encourage kids and grownups to look at the world with wonder, and hold onto that powerful, childlike ability to find pure joy in the little things. Because at the end of the day, we are all still kids growing up.

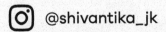 @shivantika_jk   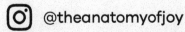 @theanatomyofjoy

a kids book about MONEY
Stromwasser

kids book about BEING INCLUSIVE
by Ashton Mota & Rebekah Bruesehoff

kids book about diversity

kids book about LEADERSHIP
by Orion Jean

a kids boo about IMMIG
by MJ Calder

a kids book about SAFETY
by Soraya Sutherlin, CEM
in partnership with JUDY

a kids book about CLIMATE CHANGE
by Zanagee Artis Olivia Greenspan

a kids book about IMAGINATION
by LEVAR BURTON

a kids book about CONFIDENCE
by Joy Cho

a kids b
by E

kids book about XIETY
szabo
and Happy Faces

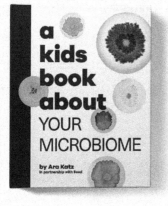
a kids book about YOUR MICROBIOME
by Ara Katz
in partnership with Seed

a kids book about racism
by Jelani Memory

a kids book about DISABILITIES
by Kristine Napper

a kids boo abo bor
by KYLE S

a kids book about DIVORCE
by Ashley Simpo

a kids book about cancer
by Dr. Kelsie Storm & Sarah Porter

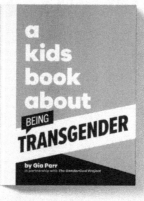
a kids book about BEING TRANSGENDER
by Gia Parr
in partnership with The GenderCool Project

a kids book about DEPRESSION
by Kileah McIlvain

a ki b a
by M

ds ok out ame

a kids book about THE TULSA RACE MASSACRE